MY FIRST ENCYCLOPEDIA

An eye-catching series of information books designed to encourage young children to find out more about the world around them. Each one is carefully prepared by a subject specialist with the help of experienced writers and educational advisers.

KINGFISHER
Kingfisher Publications Plc
New Penderel House, 283-288 High Holborn, London WC1V 7HZ

First published in paperback by Kingfisher Publications Plc 1994
2 4 6 8 10 9 7 5 3 1
1BP/0500/SF/(FR)/135MA

Originally published in hardback under the series title Young World
This edition © copyright Kingfisher Publications Plc 2000
Text & Illustrations © copyright Kingfisher Publications Plc 1992

ISBN 1 85697 260 7

Phototypeset by Waveney Typesetters, Norwich
Printed in China

How Things are Made

Kingfisher

Author
Steve Parker

Educational consultant
Barbara Reseigh

Series consultant
Brian Williams

Editor
Camilla Hallinan

Design
The Pinpoint Design Company

Illustrators
Brighton Illustration Agency (pages 14-20, 22-25,
36-39, 56-59, 98-99)
Kuo Kang Chen (page 13)
Nick Hawken (pages 26-27, 48-51, 54-55, 60-61,
74-75, 80-85, 88-91, 104-106)
Barbara Lofthouse (page 53)
Shirley Mallinson (pages 52, 76-79, 92-93)
Denis Ryan (pages 94-97)
Stephen Seymour (pages 12, 44-47, 62-65,
70-71, 114-119)
John Spires (pages 28-31, 66-69, 86-87)
Graham White (pages 32-35, 40-41, 102-103)
ZEFA (page 107)

bout this book

ng ago, most people made their own clothes, tools, rniture and dwellings. They collected food from e wild, or grew their own crops and kept a few imals. They cooked and stored food too.

day, it is very different. We buy most of the things need, from shops and stores. Often we do not ow how something is made, or what it is made m, or who made it. This book shows us, by going t into the fields and factories and workshops. explains how even a simple item such as a pencil volves the work of many people and machines. ext time you use a pencil, or eat a slice of bread, or t on a pair of jeans, you will know where it came m, and how it was made.

CONTENTS

FOOD

AT HOME

OUT AND ABOUT

From start

to finish

How things are made

Animals and plants are living things. They are part of nature. But many things are not made naturally. People make them.

People built this tall skyscraper. People made this little packet of peanuts. Who made them? What are they made of? How were they made?

This book tells you about all sorts of things and how they are made: clothes, food, things you use at home, things you see outside.

fferent things are made in different ways.

ome things are made in factories,
 people working with robots and other
achines. Other things are made by
e person at home, using small tools.
it making anything needs:

reful planning,   the right materials,

 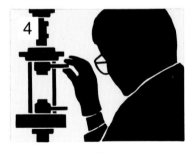

ols and machines   tests to make sure
 help,   things are made well.

🚲 Who designs a bike?

Many people take part in making a new bicycle.

The bicycle company wants to make a bike that will sell well. So market researchers ask children what kind of bikes they like best.

Engineering designers draw the new bike, to show how it will work. Graphic designer choose popular colours and patterns for it.

If the company likes the designers' plans for the new bike, models are built by hand.

These models are called prototypes. They show what the bike will look like.

he prototypes are tested to make sure the
ke is safe and works well. Then the factory
ın make thousands of bikes like it.

🚲 What is a bike made of

A bicycle has hundreds of parts, made of a
sorts of materials.

The **saddle** is made
of plastic, with foam
padding for comfort
and a vinyl cover.

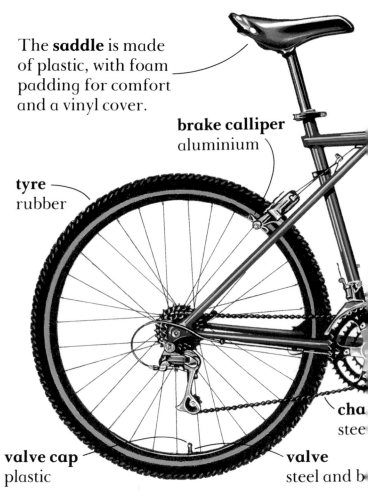

brake calliper
aluminium

tyre
rubber

cha
stee

valve cap
plastic

valve
steel and b

16

The parts come from factories in several countries around the world.

frame
metal called
chromoly – a
type of steel

handlebar grip
rubber

brake lever
steel

brake cable
steel covered in nylon

fork
chromoly

spoke
steel

wheel rim
aluminium

hub
aluminium

🚲 How is a bike made?

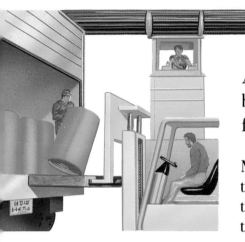

All the parts for th
bicycles arrive at th
factory.

Machines cut the lon
tubes of steel and be
them to make pieces
the frame.

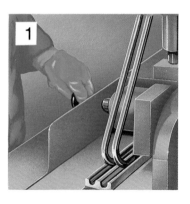

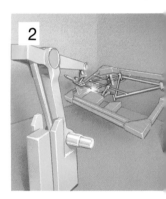

Next, the pieces are put together in the welding
shop. A robot melts small patches of metal whe
the pieces are joined together. When the metal
cools, it goes hard and holds the frame togethe

the paint shop, the frame is sprayed with
int. In another part of the factory, spoking
chines put spokes into the wheel hubs before
rims and tyres go on.

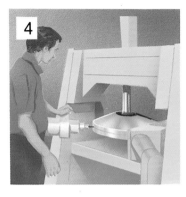

e frame is put on a moving assembly line.
ters fix the forks and wheels onto the frame.
re fitters add the handlebars and all the other
rts as the bike moves along.

🚲 Does this bike work?

A bike has to be safe, comfortable and easy to ride. And it has to last. So first the prototypes are tested. Then all bikes are tested before they leave the factory and go on sale.

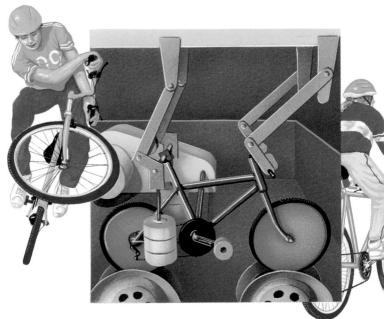

This prototype is being tested on rollers like bumpy cobblestones. A machine drives it at 40 kilometres per hour (that is how fast a car travels through a town), for 250 hours (that is about 10 days).

Clothes

♠ The fashion designer

Some jeans are baggy, others are tight.
And blue is not the only colour for jeans.
Designers decide on the style. They make
drawings of how the new jeans will look.

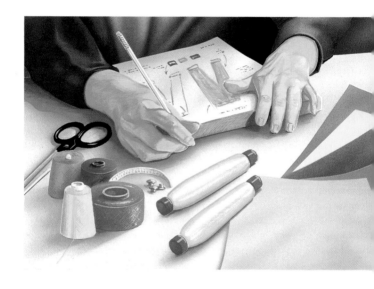

Designers' patterns show the shape of each
piece of material needed to make a pair of
jeans. Most jeans are made from a strong
type of cotton cloth called denim.

Cotton is made from the fluffy coverings of the seeds of cotton plants.

Farmers collect the fluffy bolls with cotton harvesters.

cotton boll

A pair of jeans

The cotton is cleaned and pressed into bales. The bales are taken to a cotton mill There, spinning machines twist the cotton into long threads and wind it onto reels.

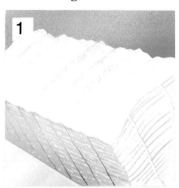

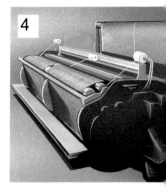

The cotton thread is soaked in huge vats o dye, to give it a blue colour called indigo. Then looms weave the thread into cloth.

the jeans factory, cutters cut several
vers of denim at once, with a long sharp
ade. A paper pattern on top shows the
ape of each piece for a pair of jeans.

hen machinists sew the pieces together.

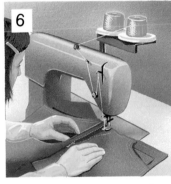

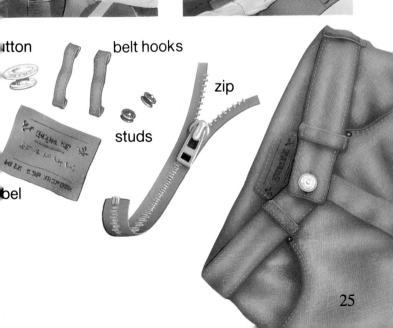

tton

belt hooks

zip

studs

bel

🧥 A woolly jumper

Woollen clothes are made from the hair of animals such as sheep. The sheep's wool is called its fleece.

The shearer cuts the wool from the sheep with sharp clippers.

Shearing is like a haircut and does not hurt. The sheep soon grows a new fleece.

...he wool is cleaned and spun into long
...reads called yarn. Then the wool is dyed
...th colour.

People buy balls of wool
for knitting clothes.

This person is follow-
ing a pattern for a
jumper. It shows her
how much wool she
needs and which kind
of knitting needles
and stitches to use.

27

⬛ Silk

silkworm

Silk is another material that comes from an animal. The silkworm is a caterpillar which spins a cocoon of silk around itself. It turns into a moth and hatches out from the cocoon.

Farmers sell the cocoons to the silk factory.

At the factory, the cocoons are unravelled, and their silk is wound into thread on reeling frames. The thread is soaked in dye and woven into cloth on a loom.

silkworm spinning

cocoon

adult moth

Silk is a beautiful material. It is used all over the world to make clothes for special occasions.

Japanese kimono, for festivals

Indian sari, for dancing

 Read the label

A label can tell you a lot about how something is made. Look at this label for a pair of jeans.

name of the manufacturers, the people who made the jeans

what they are made of

how they shou be cleaned

what size they are

where they were made

Labels appear in different places on different things.

Made of plastic

Thousands of things are made of plastic, perhaps even some of your clothes.

Plastic is made from oil.
Oil is found underground.
Giant rigs drill deep holes in
the ground. The oil flows up
the pipes inside the hole. It is
called crude oil. It goes by
pipeline or by tanker to the
oil refinery.

crude oil refinery

The refinery heats the crude oil,
to separate the chemicals in it.
These chemicals make useful
things such as petrol and plastics.

There are many kinds of plastic
– hard plastics and soft, bendy
plastics. A soft plastic called
PVC is made from one of the
chemicals in crude oil and
from salt.

salt

33

A plastic raincoat

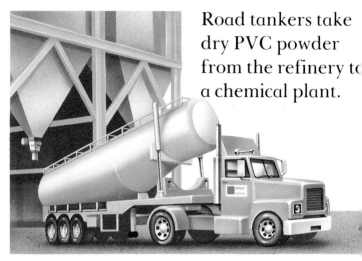

Road tankers take dry PVC powder from the refinery to a chemical plant.

chemical to make the mixture last

pigment, to add colour

PVC powder

chemical to make the mixture soft

PVC pellets

At the chemical plant, the PVC powder is mixed with other chemicals to make PVC pellets. The pellets are sold to factories that make things from PVC. Some raincoats are made from PVC.

rst, the pellets are melted into a hot liquid.

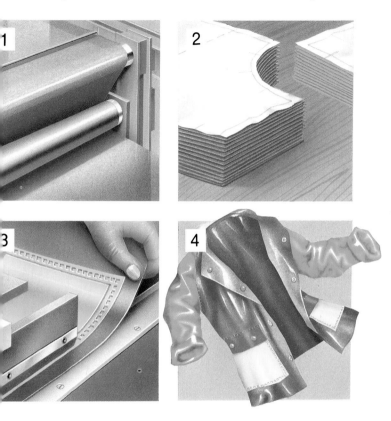

ollers press the hot plastic into a thin sheet.
he sheet hardens as it cools. Then it is cut
to pieces. Instead of being sewn together,
e pieces are pressed by a hot weight so
ey melt slightly and stick together.

🐑 Shoes

We wear shoes every day: shoes with laces and shoes with buckles; shoes made of leather and shoes made of plastic; ballet shoes and sports shoes.

Look at how many pieces there are in just one trainer. The pieces all have names.

The top of the shoe is called the upper.

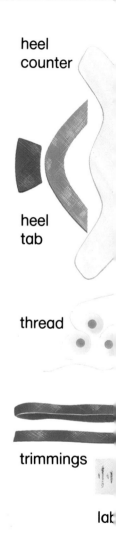

heel counter

heel tab

thread

trimmings

lab

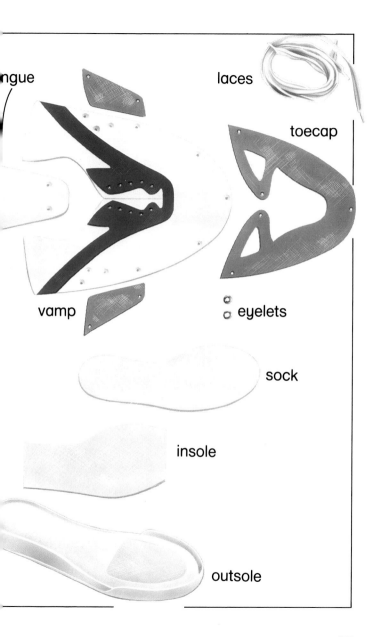

tongue

laces

toecap

vamp

eyelets

sock

insole

outsole

37

 The shoemakers

A cutter cuts out the pieces for the upper.
A machinist sews them together. Holes and
eyelets for the shoelaces are punched in.
Then another machinist attaches the insole

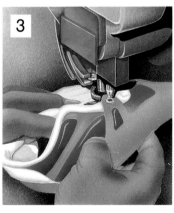

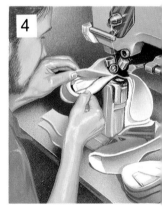

he upper is put on a model of a foot called a
st. The last is lowered into a mould which
filled with hot liquid plastic. As the plastic
ools, it becomes a hard sole for the shoe.
hen a lining called the sock is glued in.
nspectors check shoes are well made.

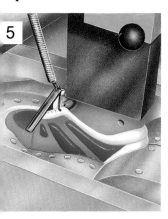

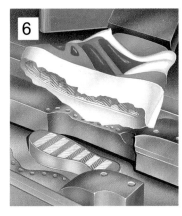

quality control inspector

 # A watch

This small watch contains 30 parts made in 5 different countries.

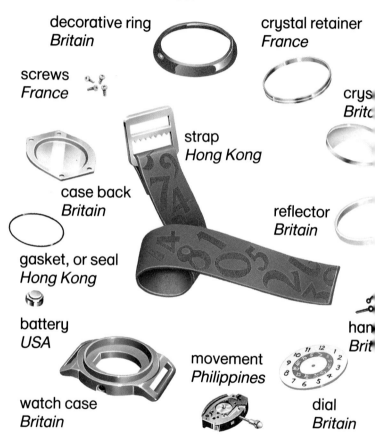

decorative ring
Britain

crystal retainer
France

screws
France

crys
Brit

strap
Hong Kong

case back
Britain

reflector
Britain

gasket, or seal
Hong Kong

battery
USA

han
Brit

movement
Philippines

watch case
Britain

dial
Britain

The movement is a set of gears and wheels whic turn the hands. The battery keeps it working.

designer draws the watch on a computer.
achines make the parts such as the dial.
hen the assembler puts them together.
magnifying lens helps him to see even
e tiniest parts.

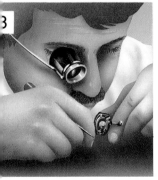

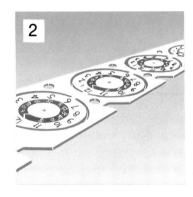

he watch is tested. It is even put in water,
make sure that it keeps working.

Amazing facts

The first denim jeans were made for cowboys, farmers and other workers in America about 100 years ago.

A good shearer can cut the fleeces of between 150 and 200 sheep in one day.

Wool comes not just from sheep but fr[o] goats, camels, yaks, llamas and rabbits too.

One silkworm can make more than 1,500 metres of silk thread in its cocoon.

Watch straps were invented about 100 years ago. Before that, people carried watches in their pockets.

Food

On the farm

Many of the foods we eat are grown on farm
and then prepared in factories. This is the
story of peanuts. In the spring, farmers
plough the fields and plant peanut seeds.

The peanuts ripen just below the surface,
inside their shells. A digger-shaker pulls
the plants out of the ground.

spreader adds fertilizers, to help the
peanut plants to grow. Like the plough and
the seed drill, the spreader is pulled by a
tractor. The plants need a lot of water while
they grow. So, during the hot summer,
an irrigator sprinkles water over the field.

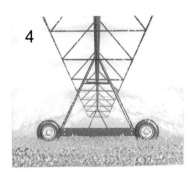

The combine pulls the peanuts off the plants
and empties them into a big trailer.
The farmer sells the peanuts to a factory.

🐄 Roasted peanuts

At the factory, the peanuts are shaken o grates so that their shells break apart an the nuts fall out.

Factory workers and electronic sorting machines check the peanuts. They take out any bad nuts and bits of shell and grit.

More machines weigh the peanuts into large sacks.

Some nuts are sold to other factories that make peanut butter and roasted peanuts.

efore peanuts are roasted, they are
metimes blanched.
lanching heats the
eanuts to make their
d skins split open.
etal rollers shake the
eanuts so their skins
ll off.

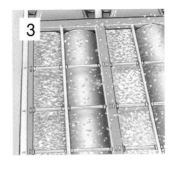

eanuts are roasted in
ot oil for about five
inutes, at 150 degrees
elsius. (An oven at
ome bakes potatoes
about the same
mperature.)

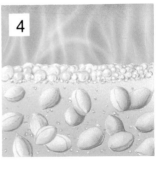

The roasted nuts
are weighed and
wrapped by a
bagging
machine.

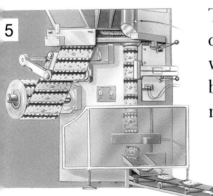

ready for the shops

Growing wheat

Most of the bread we eat is made from wheat. Farmers grow wheat in huge fields.

When the wheat is ripe, a combine harvester collects the seeds, called grain.

grain

The wheat grain is stored in huge silos until it is sold to a flour mill.

At the mill, the grain is crushed and ground into fine flour.

...nkers take the flour from the mill to ...e bakery, to be made into bread.

flour

At the bakery

Bread is often made from four main ingredients: flour, water, salt and yeast.

The ingredients are poured into a high-speed mixer.

The mixer stirs the ingredients into a soft dough. Next, a divider cuts the dough into lumps called loaves. The loaves are pu on trays and taken to a warm place called prover, to make the dough rise or swell up Then the dough is cooked in a huge hot oven, and becomes bread.

fter it is cooked, the bread is lifted off the
ays by suction pads. Some bread is sliced
nd wrapped by machine. Then van
rivers take the bread to the shops.

3

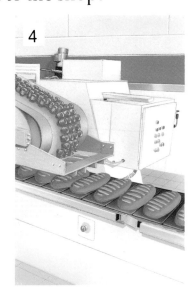

4

5

🐄 All kinds of bread

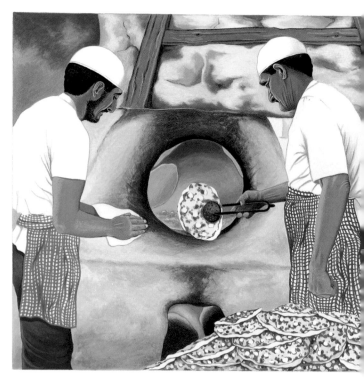

Bread can be made from different types of flour and baked in different ways. So there are many kinds of bread around the world.

These bakers are making bread by hand, and cooking it in a small oven. The bread flat because the dough has no yeast.

ave you ever eaten any of these breads?

hamburger bun

matzos

ced

roti

bagel

ta

croissant

pumpernickel

guette

pizza

ople make flour from these plants.

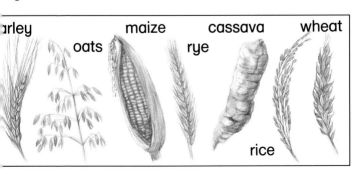

arley

oats

maize

rye

cassava

wheat

rice

🐄 Breakfast cereal

Cornflakes are ma[de]
from sweetcorn, o[r]
maize. When the
maize has ripened
in the sun, farmer[s]
harvest their crop.

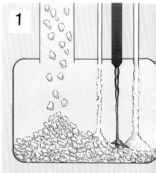

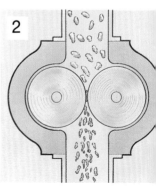

rains of corn are stripped from the plants
id taken to a cereal factory. At the
ctory, sugar, salt and malt flavouring are
lded to the corn to give it extra taste.
ext, the mixture is cooked. Then heavy
llers press the corn into flakes.

The flakes are toasted
in giant ovens, to
make them crispy.

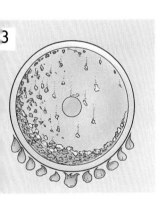

Filling machines
weigh the cornflakes
into bags. The bags
are sealed, to keep
the cornflakes fresh.

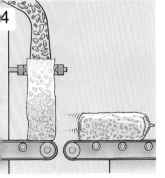

Conveyor belts take
the bags to be
packed in cartons.
The cartons are put
in big cardboard cases,
to protect them on
their way to the shops.

Milking time

Cows make milk to feed their calves. Farmers keep herds of cows to produce milk for people as well.

The cows come into the milking parlour twice a day.

lking takes about ten minutes.
e herdsman fits cups connected to pipes
er the cows' teats. When the cups gently
ueeze the teats, a milking machine sucks
e milk from each cow's udder.

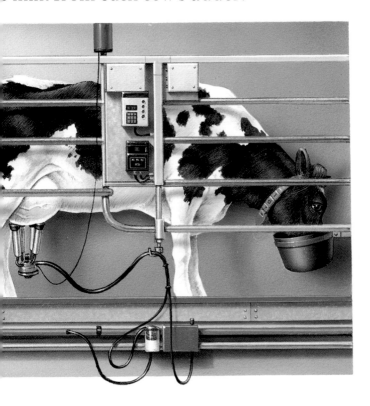

he milk flows through the pipes to a cold
nk, to keep it fresh while it is on the farm.

At the dairy

A milk tanker collects the milk from the farm each day and delivers it to a dairy.

At the dairy, technicians test samples of the milk. It must be fresh enough to sell.

t passes the tests, the milk is quickly
ated and cooled inside huge tanks. This
alled pasteurization. It kills any germs
the milk and makes it safe to drink.

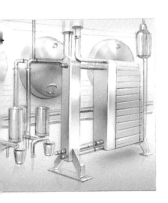

2-pint
carton

4-pint container

1-pint carton

1-pint bottle

ling machines squirt the milk into plastic
ntainers, cardboard cartons and glass bottles.

🐄 Made of milk

Milk from the dairy is used to make all of
these foods. That is why they are called
dairy products.

chocolate

ice cream

butter

Fresh Milk

yoghu

chee

cream

l over the world, farmers keep animals
at produce milk for
ople to use.

reindeer

goat

ma

camel

k

sheep

🐄 Tea

Tea plants are grown in warm, wet lands such as Asia and East Africa.

Tea pickers pull off the top leaves. The leaves are shredded and left in the air to soften until they change colour from green to brown. Then the leaves are dried and packed into chests.

Ships carry chests of tea to tea factories around the world. At the factory, a tea taster makes cups of tea from different batches of leaves. He decides on the best mixture, or blend, of leaves.

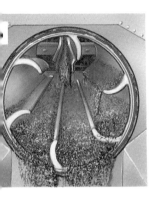

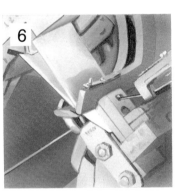

rotating drum mixes large amounts of the end. Then a bagging machine measures e leaves into pockets of tissue paper and als the edges, to make tea bags. Some tea packed in tins and boxes instead.

a nice cup of tea

Fizzy drinks

Oranges and other fruit give many fizzy drinks a delicious taste. Pickers pull the fruit from the trees.

Juice is squeezed from the fruit and packed in drums.

ips take the juice to other countries.

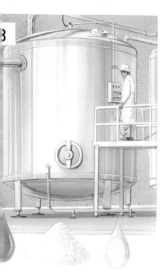

At the drinks factory, sugar, water and other ingredients are added to the juice. In a high-pressure tank, a gas called carbon dioxide is forced into the mixture, to give it sparkling bubbles.

can-filling machine squirts the drink into
)00 cans each minute. A machine called
eamer puts the lids on.

A drinks can

Cans are made of metal, often a metal called steel. Steel comes from iron ore under the ground. Miners dig up the ore.

At the steel mill, huge furnaces heat the iron ore to turn it into liquid iron and then liquid steel. As the liquid cools and hardens, rolling mills flatten it into sheets of steel. Factories buy the steel to make cans.

At the factory, a press pushes small discs out of the steel sheet. An ironing machine stretches each disc into a can shape. Printing rollers add colour. Another machine shapes the top of the can where the lid will fit.

🐄 Wrapping it up

Manufacturers, the people who make
things, package most food before it goes to
the shops. They put it in boxes and cartons,
bags and cans, jars and bottles. Some
packaging is made of plastic, some of glass
and some of paper and cardboard.

What is packaging for?
- Packaging helps to protect food and keep
it fresh.
- Packaging makes food easy to store in the
shops and easy to take home.
- Packaging helps customers to see what
they are buying. It gives them information
about what is inside.
- Food is packaged in different sizes, so
customers can buy the amount they need.

Designers plan how to package food in the best way.

Fish fingers would not fit in a bottle or a jar or a can. They might get squashed in a polythene bag.

A cardboard box is best. It is the right shape. It will protect the fish fingers. And it is not too heavy.

A plain box would look boring, and it would not show what is inside. It needs a design.

ost of the things we buy have ckaging for the same reasons.

🐄 Fish fingers

Trawler boats pull huge nets through the ocean to catch fish. Then the nets are hauled on board. Trawlermen pack the fi in boxes of ice, to keep them fresh.

sh finger manufacturers buy the fish.

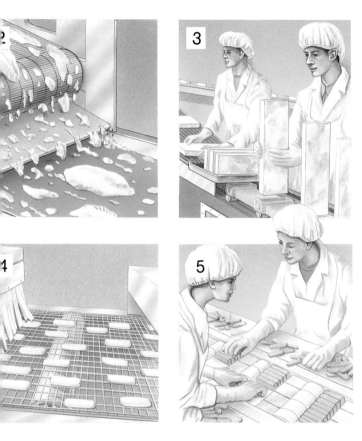

filleting machine cuts the flesh off the
ones. The fish is frozen in large blocks.
hese are sliced up, coated with bread-
rumbs, and cooked in hot oil. Packers put
ie fish fingers in boxes.

Amazing facts

Peanuts are not just good to eat. They are also used to make soap and ink!

One large bakery can make 10,000 loaves of bread each hour.

A cow can give as much as eight litres of milk in one milking.

A tea picker collects about 30 kilogram of leaves in one day. That is enough for about 20 boxes of tea bags.

In 1809, a Frenchman called Nicolas Appert was the first person to put food in cans. He won a competition to invent a wa of keeping food fresh for soldiers fighting in the Napoleonic Wars.

More sardines and pilchards are caught to eat than any other fish. Most fish fingers are made from fish called cod.

At home

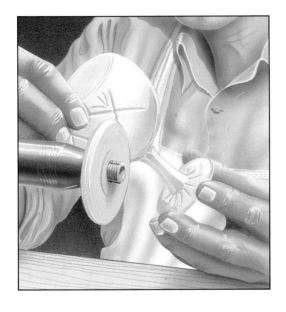

Timber, or wood, comes from trees in the forest. Lumberjacks cut down the trees wit chainsaws. Young trees are planted to replace the trees that have been cut down.

gging trucks take the wood to a sawmill.

he bark is cut away from the trunks, and
hen the wood is sawn into planks.
he wood is sold, to be made into chairs,
encils, paper and many other things.

🪑 The carpenter

Some carpenters are craftsmen and craftswomen who make chairs and other furniture out of beautiful pieces of wood.

First, the carpenter chooses which kind of wood he wants to use for a chair. Then he draws each part of the chair onto the wood

r the chair legs, the carpenter uses a lathe
turn the wood while he cuts it to the right
ape with a sharp metal gouge. Most
oodwork tools are made of metal.
ney must be kept sharp.

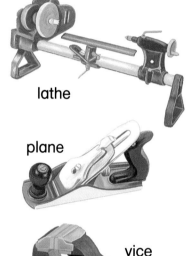

lathe

plane

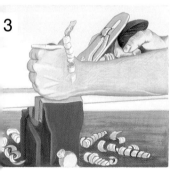

vice

he carpenter puts the wood in a vice to
old it steady. He shaves off bits of wood
ith a plane, to smooth some of the pieces.

🍵 A chair takes shape

This is the back support. A sharp drawknife cuts the wood to make the curved shape.

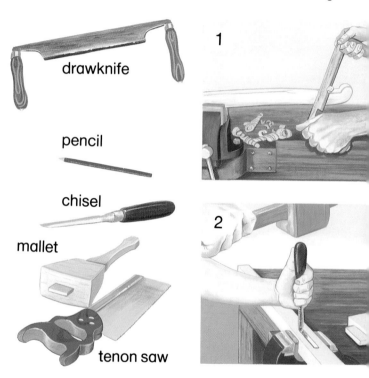

drawknife

pencil

chisel

mallet

tenon saw

The carpenter saws the ends of some pieces to make joints. On other pieces he carves a matching hole for each joint to slot into. Without joints, the chair would fall apart.

he carpenter puts some glue into the joints
d fits the pieces together. A cramp holds
e chair until the glue has dried.

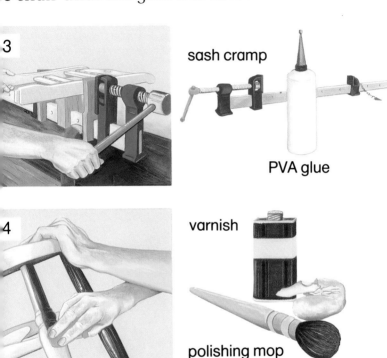

3

sash cramp

PVA glue

4

varnish

polishing mop

hen the carpenter wipes varnish onto the
air and polishes it when the varnish is
y. Varnish helps to protect the wood and
ves it a nice shine.

◗ Parts for pencils

Pencils are made of wood, clay and graphi

clay

graphite

cedar
wood

Clay lies just under the groun
Big excavators dig it out, and
blasting machines crush it int
fine powder with jets of water

80

raphite is a soft
ack rock, deep
nder the ground.

iners remove the
aphite with drills.
e wood comes from
dar trees.

◗ Making pencils

Graphite and clay are mixed into a paste. For colouring pencils, dye is added to the paste. Next, the paste is squeezed into long thin pieces called leads. Then the leads are baked until they are hard.

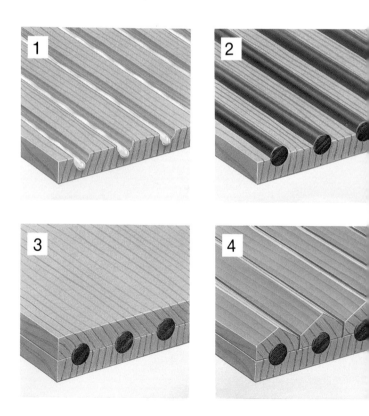

ws cut the cedar wood into pieces called
its. Glue sticks a lead into each groove in
ne slat. Another slat is glued on top.

hen the slats are sawn into separate
encils. A huge rotating frame dips
e pencils in paint to coat the wood.

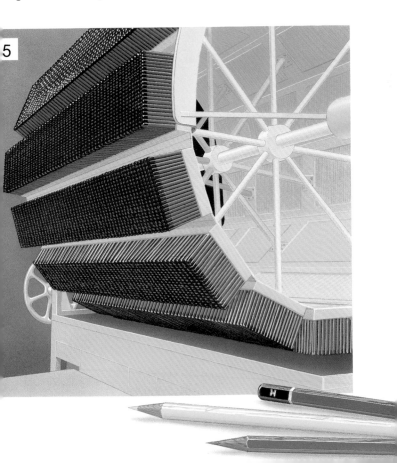

5

▶ At the paper mill

The main woods used to make paper are fir spruce and pine. This is how some paper i made. First, the bark is taken off the logs. Then chipping machines cut up the logs.

The wood chips are cooked with chemicals in a mixing machine called a digester. Thi turns the chips into a pasty pulp.

hen the pulp is cleaned and rinsed with
ater. The pulp is spread on a moving wire
reen and most of the water drips away.
eavy rollers press the pulp into a very thin
eet and squeeze out more water. Hot
llers dry the paper.

nally, the paper is wound onto a roll
lled a reel. It is sold to make stamps,
oks and many other things.

🍵 Old for new

A lot of the materials that manufacturers use are recycled materials. Recycling mean using old things again instead of throwing them away.

For example, steel is recycled. Making things with old steel helps the manufactur save money, because less new steel is used. Old ships, cars, even tins on the rubbish dump can be recycled.

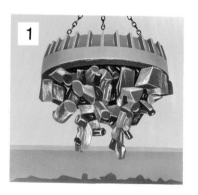

After the rubbish has been burnt, a big magnet picks out any steel cans. The cans are crushed into bales and sent to the steel mill. Old steel is called scrap.

These are some other materials that are recycled.

new plastic from old   new paper from old   new glass from old

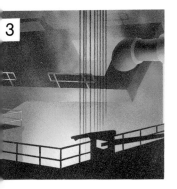

t the steel mill, the bales of scrap are
elted down in a furnace to make new
eel. A quarter of the steel in every fizzy
rinks can comes from recycled steel.

🍵 At the glassworks

The main ingredients in glass are a type of sand called silica, bits of scrap glass called cullet, soda ash and limestone. They are mixed together and heated in a furnace until they melt and turn into molten glass.

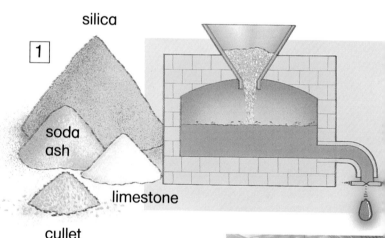

silica

1

soda ash

limestone

cullet

2

Rollers press the hot liquid glass into a flat sheet. The glass hardens as it cools. It is used to make window panes.

lass jars and bottles
e made in a
fferent way.

s the molten glass
ows from the
rnace, it is cut into
obs called gobs.
ich gob drops into
mould.

blast of air presses
e glass against the
des of this mould,
the shape of a jar.

he mould opens.
ongs pick up the jar
d put it into a big
en called a lehr.
he lehr heats the
ass again, to make
stronger.

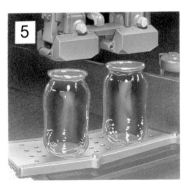

The glass blower

Some glass is made by hand. This is a skilled job.

The gatherer picks up a gob of molten glass on a long tube.

The blower blows down the tube to fill the gob with air and make it swell up like a balloon.

The blower keeps turning the tube to stop the glass dripping off. He squeezes the end of the gob with tongs, to make a long stem. The foot setter adds another gob to the stem and flattens it into a base called a foot.

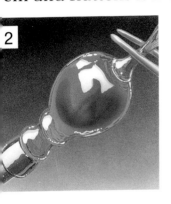

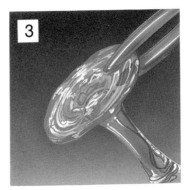

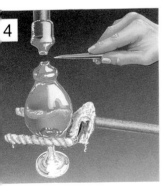

The cutter takes the glass and smooths it with a grinder. He cuts the glass with a sharp, whirring wheel to make a pattern.

Pottery

The potter puts a lump of wet clay on a fla
wheel. As the wheel turns, the potter shape
the clay with her hands. This is called
throwing. The potter here is throwing
a mug. She adds a handle.

he mug goes into an oven called a kiln.

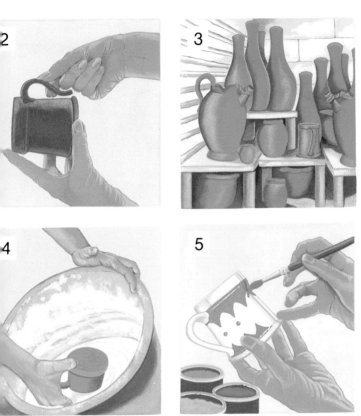

he kiln makes the clay hard by baking, or
ring, it. Then the potter coats the mug with
shiny glaze, to protect it and make it water-
roof. She fires the mug again, decorates it
ith paint, and fires it one more time.

The film crew

These people are making a programme about animals. The producer plans the story and pictures and the filming expedition. Researchers find out about the animals and the best places, or locations, for filming them.

n location, the producer and his assistant
ake sure the film crew is ready. The
presenter speaks a commentary that
tells the story. The sound recordist
tapes the sounds. The camera
operator takes the pictures. Wild
animals are shy, so they are hard to
film. The camera operator has
worked alone for months to get
good pictures.

In the television studio

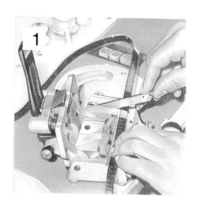

When the film crew returns from location, the camera film is developed with chemical to reveal the pictures. A film editor cuts ou strips of film that show the best scenes. She joins them together to make a good story.

sound editor chooses the tape recordings
at match the pictures.

An assistant runs the tapes while
the editor views the pictures on a
screen. He presses buttons on
the control console in front of
him to choose the right sounds.
Matching sounds and pictures is
called dubbing, or mixing.

he television programme is broadcast from
e studio. It travels as invisible signals to a
ansmitting station. Transmitters make the
gnals strong enough to reach television
erials. Now the penguins are on television!

🍵 Toothpaste

FLUORIDE

Toothpaste is made from this mixture:

● hydrated silica, to polish your teeth,

● sorbitol, made fro maize, for binding t mixture into a paste

● a foaming agent, to make the toothpaste frothy,

● mint, or other flavours, for a fresh taste and smell,

● water, to turn the mixture into a soft paste,

● and fluoride, to he prevent tooth decay

The ingredients are mixed in a vat and poured into tubes. A red light shows when each tube is full. Then the tubes are closed and packed in cartons.

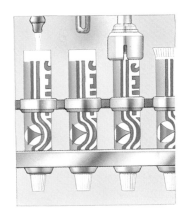

In striped toothpaste, coloured paste is put in first. Then white paste fills the rest of the tube.

When you squeeze the tube, the white paste comes out through a nozzle in the centre, and the coloured paste comes through holes around the edge.

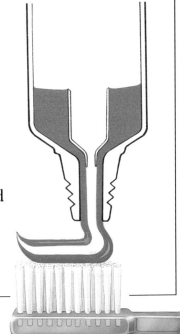

Amazing facts

▌ One pencil factory can make half a million pencils each day.

▌ The first paper was made from reed plants in Ancient Egypt over 5,000 years ago. The word paper comes from the nam of the reeds, papyrus.

▌ A big furnace contains over 400 tonnes of molten glass, which is the same weight a 10 juggernaut trucks.

▌ The first wheels ever made were potter wheels. Wheels for carts and other kinds o transport were invented later.

Out and

about

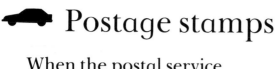 # Postage stamps

When the postal service decides to bring out a new stamp, it chooses a theme – such as birds. Then artists design the stamp.

cyan (blue)

magenta (red)

yellow

10

black

4-colour **10**

If the postal service likes a design, the artist paints artwork in colour.

The artwork is photographed onto film. A different film is made for each of the main colours. This is called reproduction.

Each film is copied onto a metal plate. The plates go to the printer.

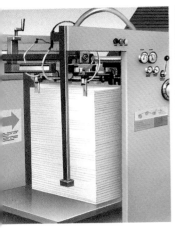

The printers load
sheets of paper into a
big machine called a
printing press. The
press copies each plate
into the paper, one
colour on top of
another. A perforating
machine pricks holes
round each stamp.
A guillotine slices the
proofs into smaller
sheets, ready for the
post office.

At the mint

Making a new coin is like making a new stamp. First of all, a theme is chosen. This coin is going to show the King of Spain

An artist designs the new coin. He designs show the pictures, number and letters on bot sides of the coin.

Look at how big the artist's drawing is. Thi is so she can fit a lot of detail into her desig for the tiny coin. The designs are sent to th mint. The mint is where coins are made.

At the mint, drawing machines copy the designs to the right size, but back to front, on two blocks of steel. The blocks are called dies.

dies

oins are made of mixtures of metals,
alled alloys. The mint buys bars of
ifferent metals. The bars are melted
a furnace and rolled into thin sheets.

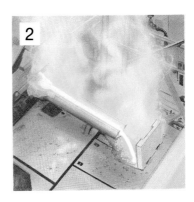

mall discs called blanks are punched out of
le sheets. Leftover metal from the sheets
oes back into the furnace, for recycling.

Striking the coin

The blanks are heated in another furnace, to make them soft. They are called blanks because they have no pattern yet.

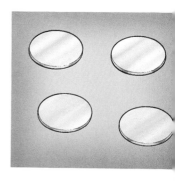

A coining press squeezes each blank between the two metal dies. The blank is soft, so each die dents the blank with its pattern. This is called striking, or minting, the coins.

quality control inspect

ll kinds of coins

ach country makes its own coins with its
wn designs. So there are many kinds of
oins – coins made of different metals,
1 many shapes and sizes,
nd worth different amounts
f money. Do you recognize
ny of these coins?

A new car

Car companies want to make new cars that
are better and more popular than the cars
already on sale. It costs a lot of money to
design and make a new car. So companies
need to know what kind of car will sell well.

Market researchers ask people what kind of
car they want. Comfortable and safe? Sleek
and speedy? Red, or another colour?

Designers make sketches
and engineers use
computers to decide
the size and shape of
the new car.

ngineers build models by hand, to see if
ans for the new car are good enough.
rst they make small models
ith clay or wood, then
odels the same size
a real car.

ext they build
rototypes with
e real materials,
test the car.

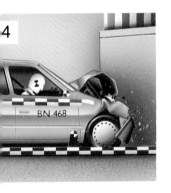

rototypes with dummies at the wheel are
rashed into walls, to see how safe the car is.
rototypes are also kept in icy-cold rooms
nd in very hot rooms, to make sure the car
vill work in bad weather.

On the assembly line

sheet steel

The main parts for the car body are made from sheet steel. A huge press shapes the steel into car doors and other parts.

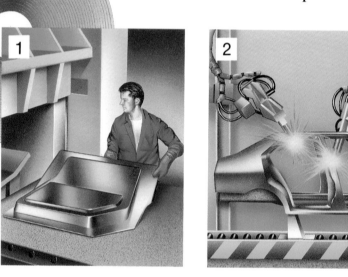

The parts are put together in the welding shop. Robots are programmed by computer to melt small patches of metal in each part. The patches stick together as the metal cools and hardens. This is called spot welding.

The moving assembly line takes the car from the welding shop to the paint shop.

First the car is dipped in a pool of anti-rust paint. Then robots spray the car with colour. A wax coating is added, to protect the paint from scratches and to make the car shiny.

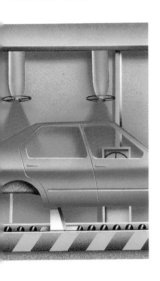
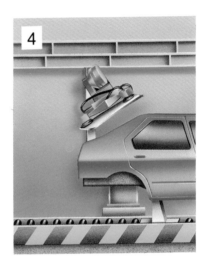

When the car comes out of the paint shop, robots with big suction pads fit the glass windscreens. Robots move like human arms and hands. They do work that is too heavy, dangerous and boring for people to do.

The fitters

As the car moves along the assembly line, assembly workers fit the other parts.

The car is lowered onto the engine and the chassis. The car is also tilted sideways.

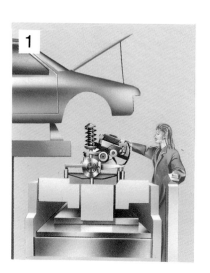

This makes it easier for fitters to connect u the fuel tank and the exhaust pipe. More fitters add dozens of other parts. At the en of the assembly line, drivers test the finishe car, to make sure it is ready to go on sale.

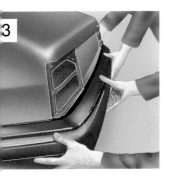

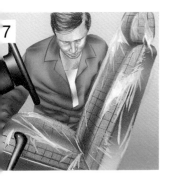

A skyscraper

Architects and planners make the drawings and desig for a new skyscrape

All the plans are checked: by people from the local area, to make sure the ne skyscraper will fit in with its surrounding by the people who a paying for the new skyscraper; and by the engineers and tl construction compa who will build it.

Model makers build miniature version, t show what the sky- scraper will look lik

urveyors measure the site. Engineers drill
to the soil and rock underneath, to check
s strength.

Demolition cranes knock
down old buildings, and
bulldozers clear away
the rubble.

On site

When the site has been cleared, building can begin. First, drills make giant holes deep in the ground.

Wet concrete and long pieces of steel are put in the holes. These are foundations to support the skyscraper above. Next, the steel frame goes up, piece by piece.

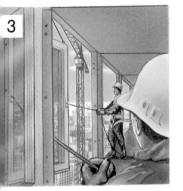

Walls and windows are fastened to the frame. Then the insides are finished.

We built it!

architect

engineer

surveyor

construction workers

takes years to build a skyscraper, and the skills of hundreds of men and women.

crane driver plumber electrician

carpenters decorator gardener

Yet building a tall skyscraper involves the same steps as making a small bike: careful planning, the right materials, tools and machines to help, and tests to make sure it is made well.

Amazing facts

Printing presses can print more than two million stamps every hour.

Silver coins are not made from silver, but from an alloy, or mixture, of the metals called copper and nickel.

A family car contains more than 20,000 parts.

The tallest skyscraper in the world is the Sears Tower in Chicago, in America. It has 110 floors and is 443 metres high.

The editor would like to thank the many companies and individuals who assisted in the preparation of this book, including the following:
Alcoa, Sue Alexander, Alfa-Laval Agri Ltd, Anglia Television Ltd, APV Baker Ltd, Atlantic Mills Ltd, BBC Natural History Unit, Berol Ltd, Boyd Line Ltd, Bovis Construction Ltd, British Paper and Board Industry Federation, The British Soft Drinks Association Ltd, British Steel plc, Britvic Soft Drinks Ltd, Camelot, CMB Packaging Technology plc, CVJ Clark Ltd, Coca-Cola and Schweppes Beverages Ltd, Elida Gibbs Ltd, European Vinyls Corporation (UK) Ltd, Fabrica Nacional de Moneda y Timbre, The Fuk Pottery, GT Bicycles, Harrison & Sons Limited, Hoechst (UK) Ltd, Japan National Tourist Organization, Kellogg Company of Great Britain Ltd, KHS Klockner Holstein Seitz Ltd, Levi Strauss (UK) Ltd, Nacanc National Dairy Council, National Peanut Council of America, The Parnham Trust, The Public Relations Business, Raleigh Industries Ltd, Rank Hovis McDougall, Renault Communications, Rockware Glass Ltd The Rolex Watch Company Limited, Royal Mail Stamps, Saab Automobile AB, Salma International Ltd, Sea Fish Industry Authority, Shilland & Co, Silk Education Service, Smith & Nephew Textiles Ltd, Staedtler (UK) Ltd, Timex Corporation, Walsall Security Printers, Josiah Wedgwood and Sons Ltd, Elaine Willis, Wimpey, Woodworking*today* and Wrangler Ltd.

NDEX